29.93   1/11

D1524802

IT'S COOL TO LEARN ABOUT COUNTRIES

Social Studies Explorer

INDIA

•● by Lucia Raatma

CHERRY LAKE PUBLISHING • ANN ARBOR, MICHIGAN

Published in the United States of America
by Cherry Lake Publishing
Ann Arbor, Michigan
www.cherrylakepublishing.com

Content Adviser: James G. Lochtefeld, PhD, Carthage College

Book design: The Design Lab

Photo credits: Cover, top, ©PBorowka/Shutterstock, Inc.; cover, bottom, back cover, pages 3,
15, 16, 23, 27, 33, 39, 40 and 48, ©iStockphoto.com/raclro; page 4, ©iStockphoto.com/ooyoo;
page 5, ©iStockphoto.com/IlexImage; page 7, ©iStockphoto.com/Mtain; page 8, ©iStockphoto.
com/travelphotographer; page 9, ©iStockphoto.com/hadynyah; pages 11, 20 and 31, © Dinodia
Images/Alamy; page 12, ©iStockphoto.com/fkienas; page 13, ©iStockphoto.com/50coyote; page
14, ©iStockphoto.com/rphotos; page15, ©ARTEKI/Shutterstock, Inc.; page 17, ©Paulprescott/
Dreamstime.com; page 21, ©AP Photo/Charles Dharapak; page 22, ©AP Photo; page 24,
©iStockphoto.com/VikramRaghuvanshi; page 25, ©Samrat35/Dreamstime.com; page 28, top,
©iStockphoto.com/OSTILL; page 28, bottom left, ©Sverlova Mariya/Shutterstock, Inc.; page 28,
bottom right, ©iStockphoto.com/h3ct02; page 29, © David Gee 1/Alamy; page 30, PhotosToGO.
com; page 32, ©iStockphoto.com/thefinalmiracle; page 34, top, ©James Phelps/Dreamstime.
com; page 34, bottom, ©AP Photo/Themba Hadebe; page 38, ©Andrea Skjold/Shutterstock, Inc.;
page 41, ©Monkey Business Images/Shutterstock, Inc.; page 42, ©Joe Gough/Shutterstock, Inc.;
page 45, ©Dean Mitchell/Dreamstime.com.

Library of Congress Cataloging-in-Publication Data
Raatma, Lucia.
  It's cool to learn about countries—India / by Lucia Raatma.
      p. cm.—(Social studies explorer)
  Includes bibliographical references and index.
  ISBN-13: 978-1-60279-824-3
  ISBN-10: 1-60279-824-9
  1. India—Juvenile literature. I. Title. II. Series.

  DS407.R24 2010
  954—dc22

                                                      2010000546

Cherry Lake Publishing would like to acknowledge the work of The Partnership for 21st
Century Skills. Please visit www.21stcenturyskills.org for more information.

Printed in the United States of America
Corporate Graphics Inc.
July 2010
CLFA07

TABLE OF CONTENTS

CHAPTER ONE

WELCOME TO INDIA!

➥ Mumbai is a thriving city that is home to millions of people.

Would you like to visit India? It is an amazing place. India has the second-largest population in the world. Nearly 1.2 billion people live there. Only China has more people. India is the world's seventh-largest country, covering 1,269,219 square miles (3,287,263 square kilometers).

That makes it approximately one-third the size of the United States. But it has four times as many people!

On your trip, you could explore the Taj Mahal. You could visit the modern city of Mumbai. Notice the **temples**—both large and small—that you see in the cities and in the countryside. You might hike through snow. You might find yourself searching for shade from the blazing sun. It all depends on when and where you go. Let's explore India!

The Taj Mahal is made of shining white marble and was completed in 1653. An emperor named Shah Jahan built it to honor his wife, Mumtaz Mahal. She died 12 years earlier. The Taj Mahal has a huge center dome, a garden, and a large reflecting pool. The tombs of Mumtaz Mahal and Shah Jahan are located inside. Thousands of tourists visit each year.

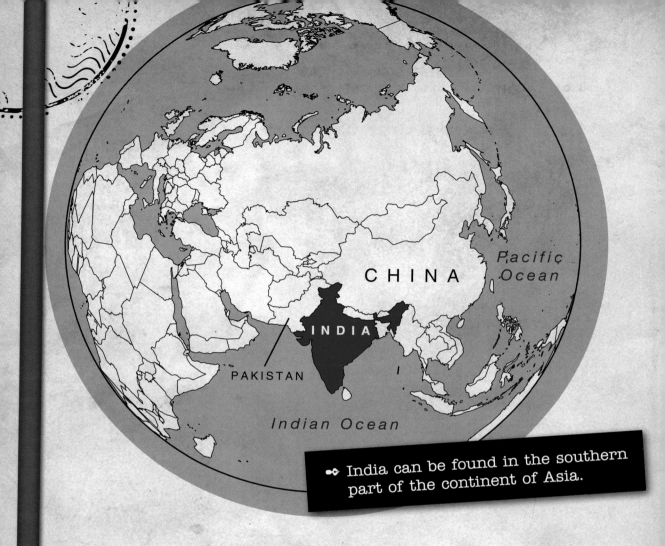

CHINA

Pacific Ocean

INDIA

PAKISTAN

Indian Ocean

◦◦ India can be found in the southern part of the continent of Asia.

Where is India? It is located on the southern part of the continent of Asia. If you look at a globe, you'll see it between Pakistan and China. India is a **peninsula**. It is nearly surrounded by water.

The country can be divided into three different areas: the Himalayas, the Northern Plains, and the Southern Peninsula. Each of these regions has different animals, plants, and weather.

The Himalayas make up a huge mountain system. These mountains stretch along India's northern border and into China and other countries. They are the tallest peaks in the world. The highest point in India is found on a mountain called Kanchenjunga at 28,209 feet (8,598 meters).

The region has villages and towns. But you won't find the crowds of people you might see in the rest of the country. Within the Himalayas is an area called Jammu and Kashmir. India, Pakistan, and China all claim or control parts of it.

➻ Some of the tallest mountains in the world are located in the Himalayas.

➥ The Thar Desert is one of the largest deserts in the world.

The Northern Plains are home to fertile farmland. Most of India's people live in this region. The capital city, New Delhi, is located here as well. Three major rivers flow through the plains: the Brahmaputra, the Yamuna, and the Ganges. The Ganges is the longest river in India.

Most of the Northern Plains have farms and forests. But the western part is different. There, you will find the Thar Desert. Few plants grow within it.

The Southern Peninsula is separated from the Northern Plains by the Vindhya mountain range. Along the eastern coast are mountains called the Eastern Ghats. Along the western coast are the Western Ghats. Both coasts have large populations. On the west coast is the city of Mumbai. It used to be called Bombay.

The Deccan **Plateau** lies in the Southern Peninsula. It has many farms, forests, and mineral deposits. The Kaveri, Krishna, and Godavari Rivers cross the plateau and provide water for farming. Along the Indian Ocean in the Southern Peninsula, you'll find the region's lowest geographical point. It lies at sea level.

➡ Tea farms are a common sight in India's southern peninsula.

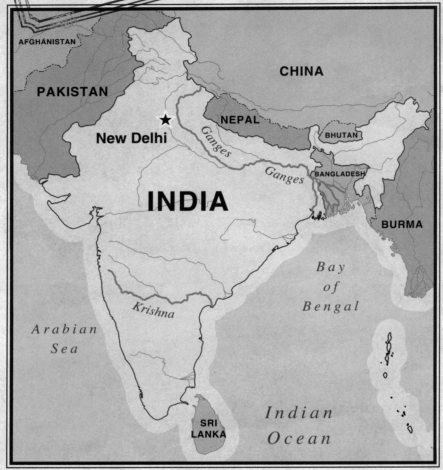

Look at the map of India above. Notice the other countries that border it. Make note of the bodies of water that surround it. On a separate piece of paper, trace the outline of the country. See where New Delhi is? Mark that city with a star on your tracing. Also label the Himalayas. Now, label the Ganges River and the Krishna River. Do you see how the Ganges River cuts across the top of India?

Hot! That's how you might feel during the warm season. This season lasts from April to June. Average temperatures in New Delhi are usually about 87 degrees Fahrenheit (31 degrees Celsius). The Thar Desert can reach a scorching 123 degrees F (51 degrees C).

The rainy season lasts from June to September. During this time, monsoons can bring heavy rainstorms. Monsoons are strong winds that blow across the Indian Ocean and parts of Asia. Rivers can flood and cause damage to farms and cities. Some parts of India get lots of rain each year. But the Thar Desert usually gets less than 10 inches (25 centimeters) of rain each year.

➨ Monsoon rainstorms can cause serious flooding in India's cities and towns.

❧ The region surrounding the Himalayas is home to India's coldest temperatures.

The cool season lasts from October to March. In New Delhi, the average temperature is approximately 58 degrees F (14 degrees C). In the Himalayas, there are frigid temperatures and snow.

If you visit India, you may see some wonderful animals. Throughout the country, there are rhinoceroses, antelopes, and wolves. There are also panthers, tigers, and lions. Freshwater dolphins and crocodiles make their home in the Ganges River. Some of India's animals are **endangered**. These include the Indian elephant and the Bengal tiger. Keep an eye out for colorful birds such as parrots and peacocks.

Bengal tigers are beautiful animals found mostly in India and Bangladesh. They live in forests and wetlands. These tigers are in danger of dying out because of hunting and loss of **habitat**. By some estimates, only about 2,000 remain in the wild. In the past few decades, the Indian government has tried to protect Bengal tigers. One way is through the creation of tiger reserves where they can live safely.

CHAPTER TWO

BUSINESS AND GOVERNMENT IN INDIA

➤ Indians work at many different jobs.

Experts estimate that India's civilization dates back more than 4,500 years. Through the years, the nation has undergone many changes. But the people of India have always worked hard. The nation's industries affect the world every day.

One of the fastest-growing parts of the economy is the service industry. Service workers provide a service instead of a product. Teachers and doctors are two types of service workers. Today, the service industry brings in more money for the nation's economy than any other business.

Have your parents ever called a company for help with your computer or its software? There is a good chance that the person who answered your questions was sitting behind a desk in India. Many well-educated, English-speaking people in India have become customer service workers for a variety of companies.

The rupee is the main type of money in India. Rupees can be coins and paper notes. One rupee equals 100 paise, much like one U.S. dollar equals 100 cents. In 2009, one U.S. dollar equaled approximately 46.7 rupees.

Some people in India work in agriculture. Most farms are small. Important crops include cotton, rice, and wheat. Farmers also grow **jute**, sugarcane, and tea. India is the world's largest producer of tea. Farmers also raise buffalo, chickens, pigs, and cattle. Though many Indian farmers will not raise beef cattle, they do raise dairy cows. Commercial fishers catch shrimp and tuna off the nation's coast.

Many people in India follow the Hindu religion. Followers of this religion believe that cows are sacred and should not be harmed. Most people in India do not eat beef, but they do use cow's milk.

◦→ The textile industry is one of many that help drive India's economy.

At one time, India's economy relied almost entirely on farming. Today, India's factories produce a variety of items. These include cars, bicycles, tools, steel, and clothing. Factories **export** carpets and other products. Many people work in the technology field, building computers and designing communications systems.

As of 2009, approximately 17.5 percent of India's people work in agriculture. Another 20 percent of the nation's labor force works in manufacturing. About 62.5 percent of India's people work in service industry jobs..

Using this information, create a bar graph that shows these parts of India's economy. Ask a teacher or other adult for help if you need it. Label the horizontal axis of the bar graph "Type of Industry." Label the vertical axis "Percentage of Indian Workers." Don't forget to label each bar with the correct industry. Which bar will be longest? Which will be shortest?

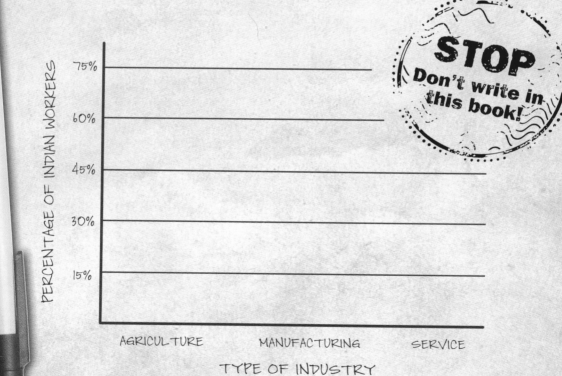

STOP
Don't write in this book!

INDIA

India is rich with natural resources, including coal and iron ore. The country is also an important producer of mica. Mica is a mineral that is used in paint and in making electronics. India also has emeralds, gold, and diamonds. These are used in beautiful jewelry that India exports to many other nations.

Do you want to know more about India's economy? Then take a look at its trading partners. Trading partners are the countries that **import** goods from a country or export goods to that country. Here is a graph showing the countries that are India's top import and export trading partners.

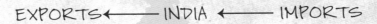

EXPORTS ← INDIA ← IMPORTS

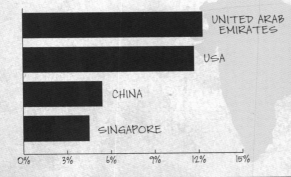

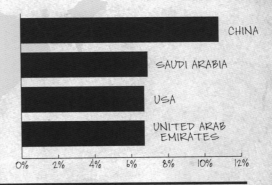

For hundreds of years, Great Britain had control of India. But in 1947, the Republic of India became an independent nation. Today, India is divided into 28 states and 7 territories. The nation has three branches of government: the executive, legislative, and judicial branches.

Mahatma Gandhi (1869–1948) played an important role in India's independence. He led peaceful protests against the British government. He often went on hunger strikes to bring attention to India's needs. He believed in nonviolence. Gandhi's birthday is a national holiday in India.

→ Manmohan Singh was elected prime minister of India in 2004.

The executive branch is made up of the president, the prime minister, and the Council of Ministers. Members of the Council of Ministers run various government departments. These officials are recommended by the prime minister and then appointed by the president.

The legislative branch is also known as the Parliament. It is made up of the Council of States and the Council of the People. Assemblies in each state and territory elect the members of the Council of States. But the people of India elect nearly all of the members of the Council of the People. A group from Parliament elects the president. Another group selects the prime minister, who is the true head of the government.

Pratibha Patil was elected president in 2007. She became India's first female president. Manmohan Singh works with her as prime minister.

Pratibha Patil

The judicial branch enforces the laws of India. It is made up of the Supreme Court and smaller courts in each state and territory. The Supreme Court has one chief justice and 25 other justices. The president appoints all of the Supreme Court justices.

India's flag was adopted in 1947. It has three horizontal stripes. One stripe is saffron (a shade of orange). One stripe is white. One stripe is green. In the center of the flag is a chakra. It is a traditional symbol from the Buddhist religion.

CHAPTER THREE

MEET THE PEOPLE

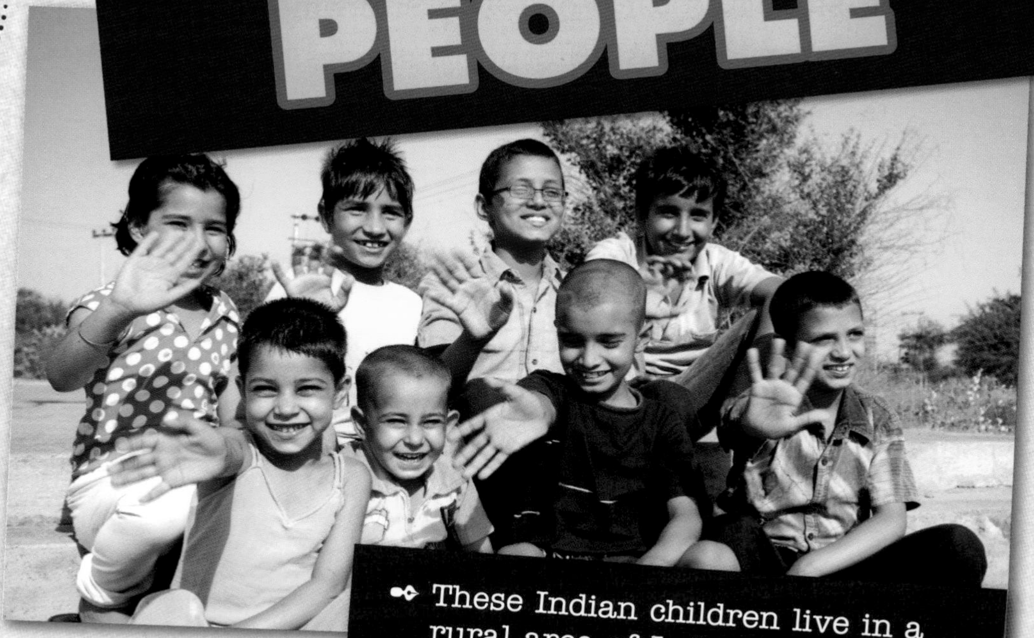

These Indian children live in a rural area of India.

India is home to many millions of people. Some people live in crowded modern cities, including Mumbai, New Delhi, Bangalore, and Kolkata. They might work in office buildings or factories. They might live in tiny apartments. Approximately 29 percent of India's people live in **urban** areas. The other 71 percent live in **rural** areas, such as villages and on small farms. They may live in houses made of straw and mud. Sometimes they do not have electricity or running water.

The people of India represent various **ethnic** backgrounds. Approximately 72 percent are Indo-Aryans. They live in the northern part of the country. Approximately 25 percent are Dravidians. They are descendants of India's earliest people. They live mostly in the southern part of the country. There are also a number of tribal groups in India. These include the Bhil and the Gond.

❧ Some Indian people live the traditional lifestyles of their ancestors.

How many languages do you think are spoken in India? One or two? Think higher! By some estimates, there are more than 1,000 languages spoken in the nation. The official language of India, however, is Hindi. Different states have different official languages, including Tamil, Urdu, Gujarati, and Punjabi. English is also an important language in India. Many people learn it.

INDIAN

Let's learn some Hindi words and phrases. Look at the lists below. On a separate sheet of paper, try to match the Hindi words with the English translations. See the answers below.

Hindi	English
1. shukriya (shook-ree-AH)	a. hello/goodbye
2. kripaya (KRI-pah-yah)	b. aunt
3. namaste (nah-maH-stay)	c. thank you
4. chachi (CHAH-cheeh)	d. grandfather
5. dada (dah-DAH)	e. please

Answers: 1-c; 2-e; 3-a; 4-b; 5-d

When you see Hindi words, they may be written using characters from the alphabet you already know. The Hindi language, however, is traditionally written in Devanagari script.

Take a look at how vowels are written in Devanagari script.

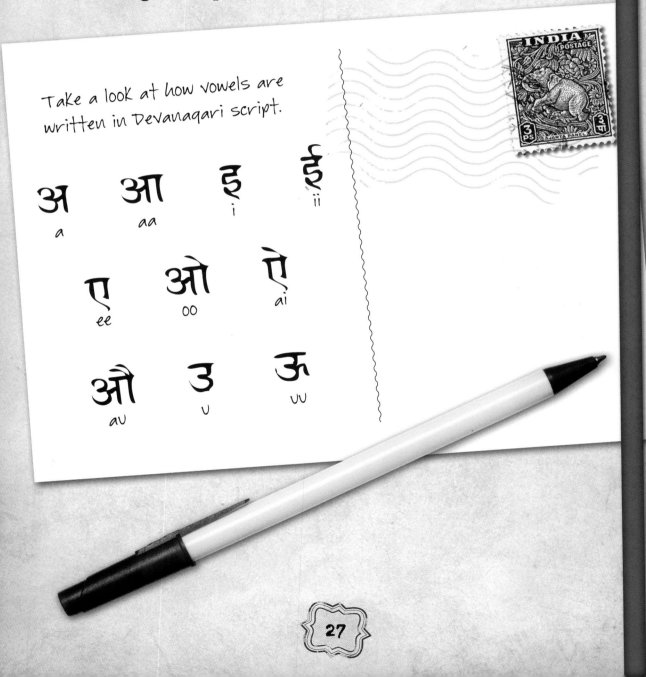

अ
a

आ
aa

इ
i

ई
ii

ए
ee

ओ
oo

ऐ
ai

औ
au

उ
u

ऊ
uu

Throughout India, family life is important. Households often include grandparents, aunts, uncles, and cousins. Religion plays a big role for many families. More than 80 percent of Indians practice Hinduism. Approximately 13 percent of India's people are Muslim. Approximately 2 percent are Christian. Other religions include Sikhism, Buddhism, and Jainism.

Vishnu

Hinduism is a religion that dates back thousands of years. Most Hindus honor many gods and goddesses. Some include Vishnu, Shiva, and Brahma. Hinduism is the third-largest religion in the world, after Christianity and Islam.

Shiva

Brahma

⚬ India's schools prepare students for a wide variety of careers.

Education in India is free for children ages 6 to 14. During those years, students attend primary school and middle school. After that, they can attend secondary school for either 2 or 4 years. Students who complete 2 years often go on to a **vocational** school. Those who complete 4 years can apply to university. This education system has produced many successful teachers, engineers, doctors, and other professionals.

Throughout India, you'll see many different types of clothing. Traditionally, a woman might wear a long, draping piece of fabric. It is called a *sari*. Saris are wrapped around the body and over the shoulder in a special way. They are brightly colored. A woman might also wear a *salwaar-kameez*. This is an outfit consisting of loose pants and a long, loose shirt. Part of a man's outfit might include a long white sheet of cloth called a *dhoti*. Today, some men and women still wear the traditional clothing. But in some big cities, they often wear Western-style clothes. These include business suits and jeans.

◦ Some Indian women wear brightly colored saris.

➥ Indian classical musician Ustad Abdul Halim Jaffer Khan plays the sitar.

The people of India have a strong appreciation for art, literature, and music. Many historic Indian paintings tell stories. Indian music often uses special instruments such as the sitar. In recent years, film has become increasingly popular in India. Bollywood (a play on the words *Hollywood* and *Bombay*) is the term given to the filmmaking industry centered in Mumbai. Today, India makes more movies per year than any other nation.

CHAPTER FOUR

CELEBRATIONS

❖ Beautiful lamps are a part of traditional Diwali celebrations

The people of India are hard workers. But what do they do for fun? They take part in holidays, sports, and games.

In India, there are lots of holidays to celebrate. Diwali is an important time for Hindus, Sikhs, and Jains. It is known as the Festival of Lights. It usually takes place in October or November. People celebrate many things and events during Diwali, including the Hindu New Year. The festival of Holi takes place in March. It marks the arrival of spring. People throw colored powder on one another. On certain days, Hindus have feasts and street fairs to honor their gods and goddesses. Muslims celebrate their religious holidays as well. Among them is Ramadan, a special time of fasting and reflection.

Here are some national holidays that are recognized in India:

January 26   Republic Day

August 15   Independence Day

October 2   Mahatma Gandhi's Birthday

India's national sport is field hockey. The most popular sport is cricket. This game is a bit like baseball. The national team has won many championships.

Athletes in India enjoy playing soccer, tennis, and many other sports. Also, some forms of martial arts originated in India.

Leander Paes

Leander Paes (1973–) and Mahesh Bhupathi (1974–) are two very successful tennis players from India. For several years, they were partners and won titles together. They have also won championships in mixed doubles and with other partners.

Mahesh Bhupathi

The practice of yoga traces its history to India. The word *yoga* is a Sanskrit term that means "union." Some aspects of yoga, especially the *asanas* (postures), have become popular throughout the world.

Many people in India also enjoy flying kites. On a breezy day, you might see dozens of colorful kites floating over fields or rooftops.

Perhaps you would like to read more books about India. If you do, get in the spirit by making a bookmark for your reading materials. Because India produces lovely gems, use colorful beads to remind yourself of the nation's beautiful jewelry.

MATERIALS:
- 20 inches (51 cm) of heavy cord
- Beads with holes that are large enough for the cord to fit through
- Ruler
- Scissors

INSTRUCTIONS:
1. Sort your beads. Decide which ones you want to use and in what order.
2. Make a knot in the cord 3 inches (8 cm) from one end.
3. String beads through the opposite end of the cord. Work them along the cord until you reach the knot. Keep adding beads until you have created a 2-inch (5-cm) section of beads.
4. Make another knot, right next to the end of the beads you have added.
5. Use the ruler to measure 10 inches (25 cm) beyond that knot. Make another knot at that point. The cord between these two knots will remain empty. This part will go between the pages of the book you're reading.

6. String beads from this third knot for 2 inches (5 cm). Make a final knot at the end of the cord, right next to the beads you have just added.

7. Trim the ends of the cord using scissors. Leave 0.5 inches (1.3 cm) of cord on each end.

Experiment with different kinds of cords and beads.

CHAPTER FIVE

WHAT'S FOR DINNER?

➤ Rice is an ingredient in many Indian dishes.

Have you ever been to an Indian restaurant? Many dishes use spices such as turmeric, cumin, garlic, and ginger.

Many people in India are vegetarian. By some estimates, less than 30 percent of India's people eat meat on a regular basis.

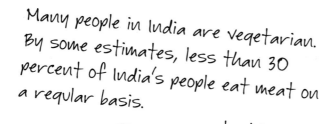

chickpeas

lentils

rice

Most Indian food relies on basic ingredients. Among these are rice and legumes. Legumes are foods such as lentils and chickpeas. The country's **cuisine** shares common elements. But dishes vary from place to place.

In northern India, dishes use a lot of dairy products, as well as lamb and goat meat. Kebabs are popular. Main courses include *tandoori* chicken. It is made by cooking the chicken in a clay oven called a *tandoor*. Favorite breads include *roti*, *paratha*, and *puri*.

Do you have a sweet tooth? You might enjoy the desserts that eastern India is known for. *Kheer* is a bit like rice pudding. This treat is often made with boiled rice, milk, sugar, and other ingredients. Food in the eastern part of India also uses fish and many vegetables.

Traditionally, people in India eat from metal plates and use the tips of their fingers. They believe that eating with your hands helps you appreciate your food.

INDIA POSTAGE
3 PS
AJANTA PANEL

INDIA

➥ Seafood dishes, some featuring shrimp, are popular in India's coastal regions.

In southern India, many dishes use pickles, coconut, and rice. Soups and stews such as *rasam* and *sambar* are very popular. *Pakora* is a fried dish made from onions, potatoes, spinach, and other ingredients.

If you visit the western part of India, you'll find different kinds of cuisines. Along the coast, many dishes use rice, coconut, and fish. Some areas are strictly vegetarian.

Throughout India, you'll find delicious, puffy bread called *naan*. It is often served with meals. A mixture of spices called curry is popular, too.

Many people in India enjoy drinking chai. This is a mixture of tea, milk, sugar, and spices. They also drink lassi. It is made from yogurt, sugar, and often fruit.

➛ Indian cooks use curry as a flavorful seasoning in many different dishes.

ACTIVITY RECIPE

There are many different Indian foods to try. Here is an easy recipe to start with. Ask an adult to help, especially with any chopping or when using appliances.

Mango Lassi

INGREDIENTS

1 cup (237 milliliters) of plain yogurt

¼ cup (59 ml) of milk

1 cup of chopped mangoes

½ cup of ice

4 teaspoons (16 grams) of sugar

ground cardamom

Instructions are on the following page →

INSTRUCTIONS

1. Wash and peel the mangoes. Carefully chop the fruit into small pieces. Remove the pit.

2. Place the yogurt, milk, mango, ice, and sugar in a blender. Blend for 2 minutes, or until smooth.

3. Pour into glasses and sprinkle cardamom on top. Enjoy!

The lassi can be kept refrigerated for 24 hours. Experiment with other fruits.

➤ Like families around the world, Indian families enjoy spending time together.

Throughout India, mealtime is important. Parents and children try to take time to sit down and enjoy a meal together.

No matter what religion they practice or language they speak, the people of India share much in common. They have a rich history, an appreciation for art and culture, and a love for their families. What's your favorite discovery about this amazing country, culture explorer?

GLOSSARY

cuisine (kwi-ZEEN) a style or way of cooking or presenting food

endangered (en-DAYN-jurd) at risk of dying out completely

ethnic (ETH-nik) having to do with a group of people who have the same culture or history

export (EK-sport) to send products to another country to be sold there

habitat (HAB-uh-tat) the place and natural conditions in which something lives

import (IM-port) to bring products into a country from another country

jute (JOOT) a strong fiber that is woven to make rope and special material

peninsula (puh-NIN-suh-luh) a section of land that sticks out from a larger land mass and is almost completely surrounded by water

plateau (pla-TOH) an area of high, flat land

rural (RUR-uhl) having to do with the country or farming

temples (TEM-puhlz) buildings used for worship

urban (UR-buhn) having to do with cities

vocational (voh-KAY-shuh-nuhl) having to do with jobs or careers, especially those that require special training

FOR MORE INFORMATION

Books

Apte, Sunita. *India*. New York: Children's Press, 2009.

McCulloch, Julie. *India*. Chicago: Heinemann Library, 2009.

Ryan, Patrick. *Welcome to India*. Mankato, MN: The Child's World, 2008.

Web Sites

BBC—The Culture Club: Festival of Holi
www.bbc.co.uk/northernireland/schools/4_11/cultureclub/learning/indiainfo.shtml
Learn about the customs and history of an Indian celebration.

National Geographic Kids—India
kids.nationalgeographic.com/Places/Find/India
Find more information about India and its people.

TIME For Kids—India—Native Lingo
www.timeforkids.com/TFK/kids/hh/goplaces/article/0,28376,610657,00.html
Check out some sound clips of Hindi phrases.

INDEX

ABOUT THE AUTHOR
Lucia Raatma has written dozens of books for young readers. Her favorite Indian dish is vegetable biryani. She and her family live in the Tampa Bay area of Florida.

J
954
R

Raatma, Lucia.

It's cool to learn
 about countries--
 India.

$29.93

DATE			

BAKER & TAYLOR